3 Day Guide to Reykjavik

A 72-hour definitive guide on what to see, eat and enjoy in Reykjavik, Iceland

3 DAY CITY GUIDES

Image use under CC-BY License via Flickr Photo Credits:
Solfar sculpture, Reykjavik seafront: Ruth Hartnup
The interior of Hallgrímskirkja church, Reykjavik, Iceland: O Palsson
View from Halgrimskirjka, Reykjavik: Christine Zenino
Bar: Christine Zenino
Garlic Roasted Langoustines: Audrey

ISBN: 1503053601
ISBN-13: 978-1503053601

"He who does not travel does not know the value of men." – Moorish proverb

.

TABLE OF CONTENTS

1: REYKJAVIK INTRODUCTION

Jón Gunnar Árnason's 1990 sculpture Sólfar ("Sun Voyager"), built to commemorate Reykjavík's 200th anniversary. Photo credit: Matito via Flickr

Reykjavik, the capital city of Iceland, is a truly mystical destination with an intriguing combination of metropolis zeal and village innocence. Known for its buzzing music scene, Iceland's capital has an enthusiastic nightlife that can give Ibiza (Europe's party capital) a run for its money.

Speckled with pub crawls as well as top-shelf bars and clubs like Kaffibarinn, the city has a wide range of nightlife offerings that will surely set your nights on fire. When the sun goes down in Reykjavik, locals flock to Laugavegur, a street where the nightlife axis of Reykjavik converges.

An epicenter of life and culture in Iceland, this city is also a paradise for cultural vultures, music lovers, art enthusiasts and history buffs. In spite of its small size, this city boasts an assemblage of fascinating cultural offerings, such as concert venues, theaters, art galleries and museums.

For those who are fond of theatrical plays and traditional Icelandic music, you can watch the impressive acts of Vesturport, Reykjavik City Theatre, and the National Theatre of Iceland.

Inclined towards art or Iceland's history? The city has a wide range of art and history museums, including Reykjavik Asmundarsafn Art Museum, National Gallery of Iceland, and the Reykjavik City Museum.

Yet, for all its energy and buzz, this city has a surprisingly unique, cozy, and laid-back ambiance that you cannot experience elsewhere in the world. If you are looking for a great place to chill out and relax, then a visit to Reykjavik can be a boon for you.

As the northernmost capital of the world, Reykjavik has a beautiful backdrop of awe-inspiring snow-topped mountains, astonishing volcanic surroundings, and a breathtaking ocean that steeps the town's toes. What's more, it has fresh air that is as clean and cold as a frosted diamond, which is why people often dub it as a true winter wonderland.

Reykjavik is quite small when compared to other European destinations. As an urban area and capital city, it only has a population of 200,000 or less. But, what the city lacks in population it makes up for with its exquisite attractions and cosmopolitan vibes that are on par with the best tourist destinations on the continent.

With its lovely setting and wealth of tourist offerings, it is no wonder hordes of travelers from all corners of the world flock to this European utopia. So, if you are looking for a one-of-a-kind destination for your next holiday trip or vacation, make sure to consider Reykjavik as one of your top options.

History

Like other Nordic destinations, the city of Reykjavik has a very interesting history. It might not be as long and well-documented as other European places, but the city's history certainly has a beguiling story. Before it was developed as a town in the earlier parts of the 18th century, the city was already inhabited by Icelanders for nearly a thousand years. Many Icelanders believed that it was Ingólfur Arnarson, a Norwegian, who first settled in this charming land. According to Icelandic folklore, Ingólfur Arnarson cast his seat pillars into the seas, and made his way to the shores of Reykjavik, making him the first permanent settler of Iceland.

View from Halgrimskirjka, Reykjavik. Photo credit: Christine Zenino via Flickr

Sound surreal and unrealistic to you? Admittedly, it's just a legend that Icelanders fabricated a few centuries ago. But, there is a touch of reality from this captivating Icelandic tale.

As many historians have suggested, Reykjavik is indeed one of Iceland's very first settlements. As a matter of fact, there are a lot of archaeological remains confirming that humans were living in this land since the year 871. Likewise, these remains suggest that the city served as a large manor farm during the first centuries of human settlement.

Reykjavik wasn't mentioned in any medieval texts or sources, except as a large farmland. However, in the 18th century, Reykjavik saw the birth of urbanization and modern culture. The Danish ruled Reykjavik and the rest of Iceland during this century.

In 1752, Frederik V, the King of Denmark, donated Reykjavik as an estate to Innréttingarnar, a firm spearheaded by an Icelandic legislator known as Skúli Magnússon. As an industrial firm, Innréttingarnar was designed to become a source of development in the country as well as a significant industrial exporter. While the firm wasn't able to achieve its high expectations and goals, it laid a good foundation for the city's industrial sector. In 1801, Reykjavik was named the capital city of Iceland.

Unlike other cities in Europe, Reykjavik experienced a boom in its economy during the Second World War. With the occupation of the UK and US, the city experienced a massive growth in employment that led to the rapid modernization and expansion of Iceland's fishing fleet. More importantly, the city didn't witness the horrors of this bloody war.

The city of Reykjavik is quite different from other capitals and destinations in the Nordic region. With its relatively short history and rapid economic growth in 20th century, the city lacks the scenic old quarters and monumental buildings that other

Nordic capitals have. Instead, this city closely resembles the cities on the east coast of Canada with their large motorways and sweeping suburbs. Nonetheless, it is a compelling city with an irresistible charm and wealth of ravishing tourist magnets. After all, it is the capital city and the focal point of tourism in Iceland.

Climate

Reykjavik has a rather capricious and unpredictable weather. One minute, you might be enjoying a warm and sunny climate, but the next minute the weather could transform into a rainy and windy autumn. Yet, for all its diversity and unpredictability in its climate, the city remains the most beloved tourist destination in the country.

Seasons

The city of Reykjavik has four seasons: summer, autumn, winter and spring. Their lovely summer season kicks off in June and ends in July, with a mild peak of 13 degrees Celsius (55 degrees Fahrenheit) and a low of below 10 degree Celsius (50 degrees Fahrenheit). From September to October, the city enjoys a cool and wet autumn season, with an average high temperature of 7 degrees Celsius (44 degrees Fahrenheit) and an average low of 2 degrees Celsius (35 degrees Fahrenheit).

Their chilly winter season starts from November and extends to March. During this season, the city experiences an average low of negative 3 degrees Celsius (26 degrees Fahrenheit) and a high of 2 degrees Celsius (35 degrees Fahrenheit). As for their spring, the city experiences a bright and dry season with rising winds during the months of April and May. The average high for this season is 6 degrees Celsius (42 degrees Fahrenheit) and its average low is 0 degrees Celsius (32 degrees Fahrenheit).

While there are a lot of snowflakes during December in Reykjavik, January is by far its coldest time of year. As for their summer, it is certainly the favorite season of nearly all dwellers in Reykjavik. Unlike most Western cities and countries, the city's summer season is relatively cool, with a temperature that ranges from 50 to 59 degrees Fahrenheit (10 to 15 degrees Celsius). Still, a lot of people in the city sport t-shirts or shorts, and enjoy sunbathing in its lush parks during their somewhat chilly summer season.

Best time to visit

When is the best time to visit this Nordic utopia? Well, Reykjavik is practically a year-round tourist hub with tons of amazing attractions that cater to all kinds of travelers. A lot of Icelanders, however, think that their summer season is the best time to visit their capital. Little do they know, this charming capital offers an endless array of things to do in winter, fall and spring. What's more, the prices for their accommodations, rentals and airfares during these seasons are significantly lower than the summer season.

On the other hand, summer there is considered their peak season for a number of good reasons. During this time, the city's daylight time reaches nearly 24 hours, truly making it a city that never sleeps. Furthermore, summertime is the best time to experience its breathtaking outdoor activities and nature trips, such as horseback riding in the Snaefelsness glacier, scuba diving in Silfra, whale-watching in Faxaflói, and cave exploring in Gjabakkahellir.

Language

As with other cities and regions in Iceland, the official language of Reykjavik is Icelandic. Since the 9th century, this language has been spoken not only by the Icelanders, but by the Nordic people in other Nordic countries as well. In addition, this language has been used in specific regions in Ireland, England and Scotland as well as some parts of Russia and France. Even though the country was ruled for centuries by foreigners, it didn't leave a great influence on their language.

Getting in

There are a number of ways you can get in this wonderful Icelandic destination. Obviously, the easiest and simplest way of going to Reykjavik is to take a plane ride. As Iceland's capital city, Reykjavik offers a couple of state-of-the-art airports, the Kelflavik International Airport and Reykjavik Airport.

Kelflavik International Airport, as the name implies, is the main international airport of the country, serving as a hub to international airlines like EasyJet, Delta Air Lines, German Wings, SAS, WOW air and Icelandiar. The Reykjavik Airport, meanwhile, is a domestic airport that offers domestic flights to Vestmannaeyjar, Akureyri, and other destinations in Iceland.

You can also get to Reykjavik by hopping on a bus, specifically if you are coming from Akureyti, South Iceland and West Iceland. But, if you are traveling from other parts of Iceland, it can be a bit overwhelming to find a bus that has a direct route to Reykjavik. In this case, your best option is to travel to the mentioned regions and get a bus ride to Iceland's capital from there. By the way, there are two bus operators that provide bus transportation to the city, namely "Reykjavik Excursions" and "Sterna."

Getting around

For the adventurous traveler, walking is a strongly recommended option since most of the city's beloved attractions and tourist magnets are located just a few meters away from the hotel areas. As you wander around the city, you'll get to lay your eyes on a first-rate pathway system, beautiful sidewalks and opulent green parks like Klambratun,

Reykjavik Botanical Gardens and a whole lot more. Not to mention, walking helps save you a few bucks from your trip to this Nordic city.

If walking is not your cup of tea, you may easily move around the city on a bicycle. While there aren't a lot of paths dedicated for bicycles here, you can get around the city legally with a bike on the sidewalk or street. A word of advice when biking around the city, get ready for a few hills and strong headwinds.

Driving is the ideal way to navigate for Reykjavik dwellers and residents. But as a tourist, it is highly recommended not to use a car as you travel about. Since most of the streets in the city are only one-way, driving here can be a bit overwhelming for anyone who isn't familiar with Reykjavik's routes.

If you are not fond of adventurous exploration, you may take a taxi cab as your means of transportation around the city. Most taxi cabs are cozy and clean, and all of them are metered. Taking a taxi cab, however, is a more expensive option than walking, biking or riding a bus.

Stræto, Reykjavik's public bus system, is reliable, clean and fast. A single ride on this public transportation system normally costs $52 or 350 KR. But if you are staying outside Reykjavik's centre, you might want to consider getting a Reykjavik Welcome card. With this card, you get complete access to the all city's buses. Also, this special card gives free access to a handful of museums as well as discounts to several hostels. Isn't this option great? To buy this special pass, take a look at the listings posted on this website, http://www.visitreykjavik.is/travel/reykjavik-welcome-card.

2: REYKJAVIK DISTRICTS

Reykjavik is the most populated city in Iceland and even though it may seem small compared to other capitals in Europe and the world, it actually manages to fit seven districts that are of a decent size. This is the so-called *Greater Reykjavik*, which includes the six nearby small towns and the town of Reykjavik. There are a few more areas that are considered as the suburb of the city, but only six of them are officialy a part of Reykjavik. Besides Reykjavik itself, these districts are Alftanes, Garoabaer, Hafnarfjörour, Kópavogur, Mosfellsbaer and Seltjarnarnes.

Alftanes

Even though it covers only a small area, Alftanes is very interesting to tourists. It is located south from Reykjavik, situated on a peninsula and this district has population of only 2,500 people. It doesn't have cultural attractions, but the nature here is what brings the visitors to Alftanes. It has a very picturesque shoreline full of ponds where different kinds of birds gather, making it a perfect place for bird watchers.

Gardabaer

The district of Gardabaer is more urban compared to Alftanes; known for its historical and cultural heritage, as well as popular events such as the annually Jazz festival. It comes as no surprise that visitors can enjoy stunning views of nature as the name of the districts translates to "garden town". Gardabaer also houses an Archeological Park and Museum of Design & Applied Arts where tourists can experience Icelandic culture and history.

Hafnarfjörour

This port town is located about 10km from Reykjavik and epitomizes a vibrant Icelandic town. It offers to tourists and locals many activities and interesting sites. It is maybe best known for the annual Viking festival celebrated by reconstructing the medieval clothes and weapons. In truth, this place has everything; a piece of history, beautiful nature and, rumors are, they even have elves. You will see here a Bonsai garden, which is the northernmost in the world and truly a magical place.

Kópavogur

The "baby seal bay", which is not only the meaning of Kópavogur but also the district's trademark. Kópavogur is mostly a residential area, but there is a thing or two that can be interesting for tourists. Smaratorg Tower is one of them, being one of the tallest buildings in Iceland, and at its base resides a shopping mall. This neighborhood also has an art and history museum and thermal pools where you can relax during your trip. Another visual highlight is the modern architecture you will find here; pay attention to the churches and the concert hall.

Mosfellsbaer

This neighborhood is best known for the fabulous outdoors. People come here for golfing, hiking and cycling, climbing, horse riding, bird watching and so on. It is a great place for recreation and it has excellent sport facilities that enable you to fully enjoy your staying here.

Seltjarnarnes

This place is known for its coastal scenery and rich birdlife. Birds are a kind of a symbol here and they are well protected. Seltjarnarnes is essentially a residential area, but Grotta is a popular recreational area for both tourists and locals. However be advised that when the tide comes, this area is cut off from the land.

Walking Tours

A great way to begin experiencing Reykjavik is a free walking tour where you will get to know the history of the city with a great tour guide. There is also a combined bus and walking tour that takes you to Seltjarnarnes and then back to Reykjavik. One of the most interesting walking tours in Reykjavik is definitely the Hidden World Walks in

Hafnarfjörour, where a guide will tell you about the legends and show you the "evidence" of elves and dwarfs existence.

Free Walking Tours
http://www.freewalkingtour.is/

Bus & Walking Tour
https://guidetoiceland.is/book-holiday-trips/a-sense-of-reykjavik

Hidden World Walks
http://www.visitreykjavik.is/hidden-world-walks

3: HOW NOT TO GET LOST

When wandering around the city, trying to see as much as possible, you might get carried away. Chasing after those elves or wondering "what could be behind that corner?" can make you later wonder *where have you ended up?*

Actually, it is hard to get lost in Reykjavik because most of the attractions are located in or around the center, so most things can to be seen are in a pretty small cicrle. For some of the long distance treks outside the city, it is better to take a guided tour.

When it comes to the city of Reykjavik, the streets and roads are generally parallel to each other. Even if you get lost, which is hardly possible, you can wander the streets and neighborhoods of Reykjavik for as long as you want without an engulfing fear that something bad could happen. Reykjavik and Iceland are known for the low level of crime and Iceland has been awarded that title seven years in a row.

If you still get lost in the city, there are key

landmarks that can help you to get back on track. From every part of the town you will be able to spot the Halgrimskirkja, which is an imposing church located on a hill above the center of Reykjavik. You can also orientate by the mountain ranges that circle around the city, but the church is maybe a better and easier option to find your way.

Finally, there is always an option of asking the locals about directions; most people in Reykjavik speak English and some speak Danish too, so if you know any of these languages, you don't have to know Icelandic to communicate with the locals. They are friendly and hospitable, and they will help you find your way.

Remember, you can always get a free map of the city in the tourist info centers. There are about 30 tourist info centers scattered all over the city, so don't worry, it is almost impossible to miss them. They usually work till 7.00pm in the summer time, while in the winter the open hours are a bit shortened, max. till 6.00pm. If you still worry about getting lost, it would be a good idea to get the city map as soon as you reach the first tourist info center and before getting lost; but seriously, once you visit you will find that your chances of getting lost in Reykjavik low.

4: AN INTOXICATING & RELAXING SIGHTSEEING TRIP

Day 1

Blue Lagoon, Iceland. Photo Credit: ryan harvey via Flickr

Despite its relatively small size, the city of Reykjavik is buzzing with amazing sights and mind-blowing attractions. From vintage art museums to off beaten paths, the city also has a fine mixture of tourist traps that will amuse any type of traveler. For the first day of your trip to this charming little capital, you should zero in on taking pictures of the astonishing sights of the city.

You'll also be able to reinvigorate your senses as you take a relaxing bath on curative geothermal waters. When nighttime comes, get a load of Iceland's awe-inspiring and otherworldly illuminations in the sky. If these ethereal illuminations are not available during your visit, watch an edifying film about Iceland at a small local cinema.

Sightseeing on the harbor

Start your trip to this buzzing capital with a blast by feasting your eyes on the animated fishing boats of the city's working harbor. Aside from watching the boats, this also gives you picturesque views of Esja peak, and the gorgeous fjord across Iceland's southwest. Of course, to see these boats and natural beauties, you need to wake up early.

Breakfast

After the harbor, take your breakfast at any of the convenience stores within the city. A great and affordable breakfast option in Reykjavik is to savor a ready-to-eat goodie in 10-11, a renowned round-the-clock convenience store. Here, you get plenty of choices, including tacos, wraps, and sandwiches. But if you are looking for fresh bread, eggs, bagels and bacon, head off to Grái Kötturin, a small café that has been a favorite of the Icelandic singer, Björk.

What are the opening hours for this trendy café?
The Grái Kötturin is open from 7:15 in the morning
and 3:00 in the afternoon during weekdays. On
weekends, the café opens around 8am and closes at
3pm.

A visit to an iconic building

For your next stop, make your way to the
Hallgrímskirkja church, one of the tallest and most
eye-catching concrete buildings in all of Europe. A
lofty and dramatic Basalt Lutheran cathedral
perched on top of a hill, this beloved Icelandic
landmark can be seen from a variety of vantage
points in the city, making it a navigational
landmark for many Icelanders and foreign tourists.

To make your visit to this unforgettable cathedral,
take an elevator ride to the top of the tower, and get
panoramic views of the city. Also, don't forget to
take a selfie on the venue with the Hallgrímskirkja
church on the background.

Additional information:

> *Opening hours: 9 am to 9 pm during July and
> August, and 9am to 5pm from September to
> June.*

> *600 Kr for tower admission.*

> *Suggested arrival time: between 9 to 9:30 am*

A splendid collection of white-marble statues

As soon as you're done polishing your photography skills in this iconic building, take a short walk to the Einar Jónsson Museum in Eiriksgata, and take a look at the exhibits displayed in the garden. As a spectator and visitor, you'll get to see the enigmatic artwork collection of Einar Jónsson, a visionary and an avant-garde thinker. As an art museum, the Einar Jónsson Museum showcases a plethora of large art-deco sculptures and other majestic artworks from this eccentric, 20th century sculptor. But, the real visual highlight of this art museum is in its garden, where stunning Gothic white-marble sculptures are displayed to the public. The best thing about this stop is that you get enjoy to everything without spending a penny.

Additional information

> *There is no need for you to go inside the museum, as you can see all the sculptors' masterpieces outside. Besides, the museum usually opens at 1 o'clock in the afternoon. The garden, however, is open to the public at any time of the day.*

> *Suggested arrival time: 10 to 11am.*

Learn more about the city's history

Billed as one of the city's top tourist attractions, the National Museum of Iceland is arguably the best and most important museum in the country. As the country's national museum, this major tourist draw entices its visitors by presenting an overview of the country's history in an exemplary Icelandic manner. From captivating interactive videos to rustic Icelandic artifacts, the museum has a dazzling array of exhibits that will give you an insight on Iceland's history from the early Viking Settlements to its impressive economic growth in the 20th century.

Additional information

> *Opening hours: 10 am to 5 pm from May 1 to September 15, and 11 am to 5 pm from September 16 to April 30.*

> *Admission fee: 1,200 KR for adults. 600 KR for students and senior citizens (67 years old and above).*

> *Suggested arrival time: 10:45 to 11:30 am.*

Discover Iceland's folk-tale monsters

To cap off an exciting and splendid morning in Reykjavik, make a stop at the National Gallery of Iceland. Get a glimpse into the country's psyche by paying a visit to this off beaten and eerie museum. In this one-of-a-kind museum, tourists get eerie visions of dead men, giants, trolls, and other Icelandic folk-tale monsters. Aside from these spooky folktale depictions, the museum also houses a wide array of paintings from 20th and 19th century artists like Nína Sæmundsson, Jóhannes Kjarval, and Ásgrímur Jónsson. Likewise, the museum boasts impressive works from Munch and the great Picasso.

Additional information

> *Opening hours: 11 am to 5 pm from Tuesday to Sunday.*

> *Admission fee: 1,000 KR.*

> *Suggested arrival time: 11:30 am onwards*

Eat your lunch

Do you feel hungry? Are you craving sumptuous culinary goodies? After your breathtaking trips to the city's beloved tourist spots, it's time to treat yourself with a filling and tasty lunch. If your stomach is grumbling for seafood staples, gormandize on the delectable offerings of Fiskmarkadurinn (the Fish Market Restaurant) in Adalstraeti. As a seafood restaurant, this restaurant boasts an innovative menu of fresh and top-quality seafood treats with Asian influences and flavors. To make your dining experience more pleasurable, the restaurant prepares their dishes in a modern and creative fashion.

Additional information

> *Opening hours: 11: 30 am to 2 pm and 6 to 11 pm.*

> *Check out their Farmer's Market menu, a menu made up of Icelandic specialties like halibut from Breiðafjörður, salmon from the Þjórsá and lobsters from Höfn.*

> *Suggested arrival time: 12 to 1:00 pm*

The world-famous Blue Lagoon

No trip to the city of Reykjavik is complete without a visit to Iceland's most famous man-made wonder, the Blue Lagoon. Nestled right in the heart of a picturesque Icelandic landscape, the Blue Lagoon is truly one of the most beautiful and popular spa complexes in the world. Besides marveling at its unrivaled beauty, a visit here allows you to relax on its geothermal steam baths and invigorating blue waters.

As a tourist in Reykjavik, you can get to the Blue Lagoon either by renting a car, getting an organized tour, or hopping on a bus. If you opt to rent car, you will have to go Route 41 (a road connecting Reykjavik to Keflavik), and move south on Route 34, Once you have traveled five miles from Route 43, move right on Route 426. Afterwards, follow the instructions provided along the way.

Taking a public bus is simpler and cheaper than

renting a car. To get there with a public bus, go to Reykjavik's BSI terminal and take the next trip to the Blue Lagoon. As for the organized tours, there are a lot of tour operators scattered around the city offering private tours to this wonderful Icelandic tourist magnet.

Additional information

> *Several bus and tour operators that provide transportation services to Blue Lagoon. For the most part, these operators transport tourists from BSI to Blue Lagoon on an hourly basis, from 8:30 in the morning to 9 in the evening. Likewise, they convey tourists from Blue Lagoon to Reykjavik from 11 am to 10 pm.*

> *Opening hours: 10 am to 8 pm.*

> *Suggested time of arrival: Between 2 to 3pm*

Northern lights

A perfect way to end a perfect day in Reykjavik is to witness an incredible natural phenomenon known as the northern lights. After enjoying your dinner in a world-class restaurant, make your way to Grótta Lighthouse or "The Golf Course," to get a good look of this astonishing phenomenon. For the most part, these lights are pretty visible from eight in the evening up to three in the morning. But take note, you have to be patient as you wait for these lights to show up. Sometimes, you will have to wait for more than three hours before these dancing neon lights will reveal themselves.

Sadly, you can only see these beautiful sky illuminations from September to October and February to March. If you are unable to visit Reykjavik during these months, you might want to consider the option mentioned below.

Watch an extraordinary film about Iceland

Tucked away in Reykjavik's Old Harbor, the Cinema No2 is a sweet, charismatic entertainment center that has been admired by many locals and foreign travelers. Often touted as one of the city's most sought-after attractions, Cinema No2 captivates it guests with its informative and interesting films like *Birth of an island - The Making of Iceland* and *Chasing the Northern Lights*. From Iceland's volcanic eruptions to the scintillating northern lights, these films give you an extensive insight on the country's most precious jewels and places. If you are interested in watching a film from this lovely cinema center, just be there before eight in the evening.

For schedules and more information about their films, just refer to their official website at http://www.thecinema.is/.

5: THE GOLDEN CIRCLE ROUTE

Day 2

Gulfoss Waterfall, Iceland. Photo credit: <u>Dan Heap</u> via Flickr

After waking up, stretch your legs and get ready for a new day of fun and adventure. For the second day of your trip to Reykjavik, you will be going on a spellbinding journey that will take you to the most spectacular natural wonders of Iceland. As the sun goes down, you will be heading to Laugavegur, the focal point of Reykjavik's nightlife.

Why should I take the Golden Circle Route?

The Golden Circle Route is a legendary tourist route that gives you a chance to experience the countryside charm of Iceland as well as take snapshots of its most spectacular landscapes and natural wonders. A 190-mile journey, the Golden Circle Route could very well be the highlight of your trip to this idyllic heavenly European city. From immaculate white glaciers to gushing geysers, get ready to be mesmerized by breathtaking natural spectacles that can only be found in this Nordic country. Sound fun to you? Then don't forget to include this trip in your travel itinerary.

What are my options for this tourist route?

As a tourist of this scenic city, you can easily pay homage to the route's main attractions by a tour bus or a rented car. While driving with a rented car can be a great and economical option for most Icelanders, it is best for foreign travelers to take this route with a tour company. Renting a car may offer you flexibility, but taking a bus tour is more convenient. Not to mention, the roads for these routes are a bit slippery, which can be quite dangerous for drivers who are not familiar with the territory. In any season, the roads for these routes are wet and moist caused by Iceland's snowflakes and foggy temperature.

Tour operators

There are a lot of operators that offer tours for this fabled tourist route. But as a tourist, you should only choose between Iceland Horizon and Iceland Excursions. These operators are considered the best by many travelers when it comes to providing tours to Golden Circle Route.

Iceland Horizon

A family-operated tour company, the Iceland Horizon is, without a doubt, one of the most popular tour operators in the city of Reykjavik. As a leading tour operator, the Iceland Horizon is more than just a means of transport, as they keep your travel experiences more fun, friendly and personal.

Address: Granaskjol 38, Reykjavik, Iceland

Contact number: +354 866 7237

Price per tourist: 9,000 KR

Website: http://www.icelandhorizon.is/

Iceland Excursions

With over 25 years of experience in Icelandic tourism, it is no wonder a lot of travelers choose Iceland Excursions as their tour operator to the Golden Circle Route. A licensed travel agency, Iceland Excursions is truly a leading specialist in Iccland's tourism sector. Furthermore, it has a fleet of cutting-edge tour buses that come in array of sizes.

Address: Hafnarstraeti 20, 101 Reykjavik, Iceland

Contact number: +354 540 1313

Price per tourist: 8,500 to 9,500 KR

Website: http://www.grayline.is/

Highlights of the Golden Circle Route

Your Golden Circle Route tour will make its first stop at a historic site known as Thingvellir National Park. A UNESCO World Heritage Site, the Thingvellir National Park is a host to the longest operating parliament in the world, which was founded in 930 AD. Furthermore, the site boasts a dramatic and interesting landscape in which the tectonic plates of North America and Europe meet.

From the Thingvellir National Park, you will be travelling towards the next stop, which is the Geyser Geothermal area. As your bus moves to the next tourist magnet, take a few snapshots of Iceland's amazing and timeless rugged terrains. The landscapes you will pass during your trip are nothing short of ~~amazing~~ epic. So, make sure that you have an extra digital storage card for your camera or mobile phone, as you take pictures of Iceland's head-turning natural sights.

A trip to the Golden Circle Route takes you to one of Iceland's most sought-after tourist magnets, the Geysir, also referred as "The Great Geysir." Known as the father of all geysers, this historic natural spectacle is the first ever discovered geyser in the world, giving its term to geysers all over the world.

Although the site's main geyser doesn't erupt frequently, Strokkur (the smaller geyser), gushes jets of torrid water in air every eight minutes or so. Aside from Geysir and Strokkur, there are a few other small geysers bubbling on the site as well.

Aptly named as the "Golden Falls," the Gullfoss is a hypnotizing sight that will surely leave its spectators in awe. A striking, colossal, two-tiered waterfall, this majestic natural wonder has been a staple in many Golden Circle Route tours. As you marvel at this gigantic Icelandic beauty, you get a chance to see an endless flow of glacial water crashing into a rift, with mists rising visibly for miles. Indeed, the beauty and force of this stunning waterfall are things your camera would want to linger on. What's more, your ears will be treated with the captivating thunderous sounds of the falls.

The Gullfoss is also a great place to take your lunch. Tourists usually head to the Gullfoss café to savor delectable lunch meals and treats. In some cases, though, a stop will be made for a lunch break at the Information Center in the Geysir Geothermal area.

From the Golden Waterfalls, you will be setting your sights to the next attractions of the trip that may include the Skalholt Church, Mt. Hengil Volcano, Langjkull Glacier and Hverageroi.

6: TIME TO PARTY

Day 2: Night

Kaffibarinn. Photo credit: <u>Neil MacWilliams</u> via Flickr

With the second day of your Reykjavik trip already
in the books, it is time for you to party and get a
taste of the city's much-publicized nightlife scene.
Heralded as one of the world's hottest place to
party, the city of Reykjavik has a multitude of
different nightlife offerings, from live bands and

disco clubs to cozy pubs and luxurious lounges. To top it off, the city has high-quality local beers and strong Icelandic schnapps.

The focal point of Reykjavik's nightlife is on its main street, Laugavegur. Here, party animals get to pick their poison from over fifty intoxicating nightlife venues. But with so many options available, how can you pick the right place to party in this dynamic Nordic capital? Luckily for you, this travel guide has a handful of suggestions that will help you choose the best places to spend your late evenings in the city of Reykjavik.

Kaffibarinn: The Trendiest Night Spot in Town

This nightlife venue might be bit small for your taste, but Kaffibarinn is certainly the standard-bearer of Reykjavik's nightlife. As a matter of fact, many people even think that Kaffibarinn is the venue responsible for making the city's reputation as a party capital. Featuring a trendy bohemian vibe, the bar is truly a cozy gem with hyper-cool electronic music, beautiful people, delicious cocktails, frozen bottles of beer and stylish decorations. If you want to experience the essence of Icelandic nightlife, the Kaffibarinn is your best bet.

Additional information:

> *Opening hours: 4:30 pm to 1:00 am from Sunday to Thursday. 5:00 pm to 4:30 am on*

Fridays and Saturdays.

Address: Bergstadastraeti 1, Reykjavik, Iceland

Contact number: +354 551 1588

Dillon Whiskey Bar: Fine Whiskeys with Classic Rock Music

Do you love whiskeys? If your answer is yes, then take time to drop by the Dillon Whiskey Bar. Known as Iceland's largest whiskey bar, the Dillon Whiskey Bar has an endless selection of beers and of course, whiskies. Apart from its mind-blowing drinks, the venue also plays cool classic rock tunes from the city's finest and trendiest rock bands and musicians. On top of it all, the place has a rustic and amazing ambiance.

Additional information

Opening hours: 2 pm to 1 am from Sunday to Thursday. 2 pm to 3 am on Fridays and Saturdays.

Address: Laugarvegur 30, 101 Reykjavik, Iceland

+354 578 2411

Café Oliver: A Zesty Dance Club by Night

One of the latest cafes in the city, Café Oliver is a top-notch restaurant that serves a sumptuous array of Icelandic staples and dishes. But as nighttime comes, this 3-floor café magically transforms into a dance club dotted with sweaty people dancing to the heart-pounding beats of the DJ. Not to mention, the place serves a wide variety of fine alcoholic drinks.

Additional information

> *Opening hours: 11 am to 1 am from Monday to Thursday. 11 am to 4:30 am on Fridays. 10 am to 4:30 am on Saturdays. 10 am to 1 am on Sundays.*

> *Address: Laugavegi 20a, Reykjavik, Iceland*

> *Contact number: +354 552 2300*

Lebowski Bar: A Cushy and Modish Themed Bar

Does the name ring a bell? Of course, this cool Icelandic bar is named after the famous 1998 comedy film 'The Big Legowski.' As you would expect, the bar has a cushy and stylish interior space that was designed after the said film. From the bowling alley and carpets to the Americana, this joint has the coolest bar theme in all of Iceland. In addition to its classy decorations, the venue is quite known for its beers, milkshakes and big juicy burgers.

Additional information

> *Opening hours: 11 am to 1 am from Sunday to Thursday. 11 am to 4 pm on Fridays and Saturdays.*

> *Address: Laugarvegur 20a, 101 Reykjavik, Iceland*

> *Contact number: +354 552 2300*

English Pub: A Classy Bar with a twist

The English Pub is a classy and unique pub that serves more than 30 of the finest brands of whiskey, ale and beer to the thirsty party-holics of the city. It also features a game called 'wheel of fortune,' where a guest can win a meter of high-quality beer. To top it all off, the pub spotlights troubadours and cover bands, playing catchy tunes that appeal to all kinds of party goers.

Additional information

> *Opening hours: 12 pm to 1 am from Sunday to Thursday. 12 pm to 5 am on Fridays on Saturdays.*

> *Address: Austerstraeti 12A, Reykjavik, Iceland*

Contact number: +354 578 0400

Boston: A Relaxing Nightlife Offering

Thanks to its vintage and relaxing environment, Boston has become a favorite place to hang out for people who want to chill out and catch up with their companions. A breath of fresh air in the city's nightlife scene, Boston has a very laid-back vibe coupled with a stylish interior embellished with antique furniture, glass mosaics, and animal trophies. To make its ambiance more dramatic and tranquilizing, the venue provides soft lighting effects and an engaging blend of oldies and jazz music. On the second floor of the bar, there is a rustic patio where guests can enjoy stunning views of the old city.

Additional information

> *Opening hours: 7 pm to 1 am on Sundays. 4 pm to 1 am from Monday to Thursday. 4 pm to 3 am on Fridays and Saturdays.*

> *Address: Laugarvegur 28b, Reykjavik, Iceland*

> *Contact number: +354 517 7816*

These are just some of the numerous nightlife offerings of this trendy Icelandic city. If you are an adventurous party animal, you may try the other lesser known nightlife centers of the city.

Helpful tips

Most clubs, bars and lounges in Reykjavik can be accessed for free. But, expect to pay a few bucks to enter live music events and venues.

The minimum drinking age in this city is twenty years old. If you look a tad younger than that, make sure to bring with you an ID, or better yet, your passport.

Weekends are the best time to party in this buzzing capital. Not only will the clubs feature renowned musicians during weekends, but they will also extend their party hours.

7: SHOPPING & CULTURE IMMERSION

Day 3

Laugavegur. Photo credit: Jonas Forth via Flickr

Looking for vintage fashion items and unique Icelandic souvenirs to bring back home? Well, today may be your luck day. On the third day of your mesmerizing trip to Reykjavik, you will be visiting the city's most chic and sought-after shopping centers and boutiques. Likewise, you will be making a quick stop to a large shopping mall or a convivial flea market. To end your trip in the city of Reykjavik on a high note, you should immerse yourself into the kaleidoscopic and marvelous culture of the city.

Shopping scene in Reykjavik

Reykjavik is truly a godsend for luxurious travelers and shopaholics. Known as a shopper's paradise, the city is dotted with renowned international clothing brand names. What's more, the city is home to dozens of enigmatic fashion shops, premium quality art studios, and talented Icelandic fashion designers.

Shopping in Reykjavik, however, goes beyond buying elegant fashion items and well-known international clothing brands. With the Icelanders' creativity and ability to fabricate captivating and unique souvenirs, the city of Reykjavik also features a wealth of local souvenir stores that sell classic Icelandic jewelry, art and clothing. The best thing about these local Icelandic souvenir stores is that they sell high-quality items at very affordable and reasonable prices.

Important notes when shopping in Reykjavik

Shopping hours in this Icelandic destination vary, but most shops and shopping centers open at 10 o'clock in the morning and close at 6 in the evening. On weekends, nearly all shops have shorter opening hours.

Don't forget to reclaim a 15-percent VAT (or "Value Added Tax") refund for every purchase.

Downtown shopping in the city

Start your day to this glamorous shopping heaven with an element of excitement by wandering around its main shopping street, Laugavegur. Located in the downtown area of Reykjavik, this famous shopping center is teeming with classy and renowned international chains like Debenhams and Zara.

As you make your away around Laugavegur, you'll get to discover an assemblage of gorgeous shops and charming boutiques where you will find fashion treasures that range from the golden era's vintage classics to the concept-driver and ultra-modern clothing.

Aside from buying and window shopping, there are a couple of other ways to enjoy your much-anticipated visit to this buzzing shopping street. For one, you may enjoy a toothsome and tasty breakfast at any of its breakfast joints, such as Fru Berglaugand Grái Kötturinn, Prikið Bar, and Kaffitár. More importantly, a visit here evokes you to experience the shopping culture of the Icelanders.

After shopping and wandering around the main retail street of Reykjavik, head down to Skólavödustígur, a street that leads from Laugavegur to the iconic Hallgrimskirkj church.

Often overlooked for its neighboring street, Laugavegur, this street has been a trendy and popular shopping area lately. Here, customers get to visit a heap of stores that sell ultra-fashionable outdoor equipment and wear, such as the Snorrabraut 60.

Additional information

> *Recommend time of arrival: 8am to 10:30am*

> *Except for the breakfast joints, stores in the downtown area normally open at 10am in the morning.*

Are you looking for an antique lamp or a vegetable knife? Do you want to sample a fermented shark or dried fish? Whatever it is you are looking for, you are most likely to find it in Kolaportið, the only flea market in Iceland. Nestled in an old building near the Reykjavik harbor, this bustling flea market is a place where Icelanders and foreign tourists of all ages gather on the weekends to hunt for hidden treasures, antiques, books, old garments, artifacts, toys and many more.

Do you feel hungry? The flea market sells edible stuff and delicious Icelandic delicacies such as: hangikjot, skyr, bollur and kleinur. Likewise, there is a cafeteria available, as well as a famous hot dog stand nearby known as Bæjarins Beztu.

Additional information:

Address: Laugardalur 24, Reykjavik, Iceland

Opening hours: 10am to 5pm on Saturdays and 11am to 5m on Sundays

Suggested time of arrival: 11am to 12:30pm

Unfortunately for some tourists, this dynamic and lively flea market is only open on weekends. If you are unable to visit the city on a weekend, consider the option mentioned below.

A stop at one of the biggest shopping malls in Iceland

As soon as you are done shopping in the city's downtown area, make your way to Smaralind, the newest shopping mall to hit the city. With over a hundred shops available, Smaralind is without question one of the largest shopping malls in Iceland. Besides its comprehensive collection of shops, the mall also has relaxing lightning effects, beautiful architecture and a cozy plaza setting.

In this large, beautiful mall, visitors will find a broad collection of famous international brands. As one of Iceland's hippest and biggest shopping plazas, Smaralind houses several distinguished international brands with the likes of Ecco, Joe Boxer, Dressmann, Jack & Jones, Dorothy Perkins, Nike, Evans, Malene Birger, Apple, Topshop, Zara,

Benetton, Hugo Boss, and a whole lot more.

Smaralind, however, is more than just a shopping center. As you visit here, you may take your lunch in any of its world-class restaurants and cafes, such as TGI Friday's. Are in the mood for something sweet? Try to hit up to any of the ice-cream stores and desert stations within the mall.

Smaralind is also a great place to socialize with the Icelanders, create new pleasing memories, and learn more about the city's culture. There are cultural events that take place on a regular basis in this shopping mall, including musical numbers, fashion shows and even pop-up markets.

Business hours:

11am to 7pm: Monday to Wednesday

11am to 9pm: Thursday

11am to 7pm: Friday

11am to 6pm: Saturday

1pm to 6pm: Sunday

Additional information:

Address: Smárar, Kopavogur, Iceland

The best time to visit this Icelandic mall is from 11:30 am to 1:30 pm. That way, you can enjoy a filling lunch at any of its restaurants as well as experience some of its entertainment options.

Learn more about the city's highly acclaimed music scene

Get a closer look at Iceland's culture and music scene with a stop at the 12 Tonar, one of the highly recommended attractions in Reykjavik. A visit here entails browsing through a fantastic collection of music, by both foreign and local musicians. Furthermore, it allows you to enjoy a delightful cup of coffee while talking to the knowledgeable dude who runs the place.

Additional information:

> *Address: Skólavörðustígur 15, 101 Reykjavík, Iceland*

> *Contact number: +354 511 5656*

> *Opening hours: 10am to 6pm from Monday to Fridays, and 10am to 4pm on Saturdays. Sundays are close during the winter season, but they are open daily during the other seasons.*

> *Recommended time of arrival: 2:30 to 3pm*

Visit the Reykjavik City Library

To learn more about the city's history and culture, drop by the Reykjavik City Library. A cultural sanctuary, the Reykjavik City Library has a wide array of exhibits that will give you a glimpse of the Icelandic culture. Known for it's diverse book collection, the venue has a free, bewitching photography museum as well.

Additional information:

> *Address: Grofarhus, Tryggvagata 15, Reykjavik, Iceland*

> *Contact number: +354 411 6100*

> *Opening hours may vary depending on the showcased exhibits. But for the most part, they are open from 8am to 6pm.*

> *Recommended time of arrival: 3 to 4pm*

> *If the library is unavailable during your visit to the city, make your way to Volcano House.*

Watch a film

One of the best ways to end an unforgettable getaway in Reykjavik is to watch an educative documentary about Iceland's volcanoes at Volcano House. Billed as one of the most celebrated cultural attractions of Reykjavik, the Volcano House is a simple, yet renowned cinema that showcases high-quality movies about the volcanoes of the country.

Furthermore, the place has a souvenir shop as well as a collection of lava stones and exquisite artworks from several well-known Icelandic artists.

Additional information:

Address: Tryggvagata 11, Reykjavik 101, Iceland

Contact number: +354 555 1900

Opening hours: Open every day from 10:00 am to 9:00pm

Recommended time of arrival: 5pm to 6pm

8: REYKJAVIK'S LOCAL CUISINE

As a fishermen's country, Iceland is widely known for seafood specialties, however it is also for the extraordinary lamb. In fact, most of their traditional dishes are meat-based with vegetables as the side dish. There are some types of dishes that Icelanders consider delicacies, that perhaps for foreigners would seem an uneatable type of weird. With that said, here are a few that you may want to give a try.

Smoked lamb or hangikjöt is one of the dishes you must taste; the flavor is extraordinary and nothing like the smoked lamb you may have tasted elsewhere. The secret is that Icelanders leave their sheep free to climb the highlands and in the fall they go and collect them. The lamb is smoked in an old-fashioned way and the combination of all these steps makes it one of the tastiest dishes in Iceland. Another lamb dish is svið, which is boiled sheep head served with mashed potatoes and carrots.

When it comes to seafood, there are various specialties that you can encounter in Iceland and Reykjavik, but the most popular are trout, salmon, lobster and herrings. Probably the most unusual seafood dish is Hákarl, which is actually Greenland Shark that is toxic if eaten fresh, so they bury it in the ground for about six month to make it less toxic. It is a very unusual dish and not many can handle the taste of this meat; sample in small quantities.

Certain types of birds are considered a specialty as well, such as puffins. It is hard to imagine eating that cute little bird, but surprisingly, their meat tastes very good smoked. When it comes to desserts, you should try skyr. It's a little like yogurt and it can be found fruit flavoured, mostly with berries that are popular in the Iceland, and also plain.

Drinks are not much different from the norm; and you will readily find enjoyable coffee, tea and water. But, when it comes to alcohol, the most popular drink is probably beer, taking into account that they had almost a century long prohibition of beer in Iceland. However, a traditional alcohol drink that you should definitely try, but watch your limits, is brennivín, a type of their schnapps made of potatoes and caraway seeds. This drink also carries a famous nickname svarti dauði or "black death". Again, sample in small quantities.

If you want the guided food tours that will help you to pick your favorite dish, there is a Reykjavik Food Tour that will lead you through restaurants and gourmet shops in the city that will give you samples of different local specialties. If you want something more, with the beverage included in the tour, you can choose Eskimos culinary tour. For those who would like to learn how to cook some of these Icelandic dishes, there are cooking classes provided by Salt Eldhus Cooking School. You will get to have fun, cook with supervisors and taste the dishes that you have created.

Reykjavik Food Tour

http://reykjavikfoodtour.com/

Eskimos Culinary Tour
http://www.iceland.eskimos.is/Viewproduct/reykjavik-culinary-food-city-tours-iceland

Salt Eldhus Cooking School
http://www.visitreykjavik.is/salt-eldhus

9: WHERE TO EAT?

Reykjavik, Iceland. Photo credit: sharlenechiu via Flickr

Are you in the mood for eating spicy Asian dishes? Are you looking for high quality seafood delicacies? Well, fear not, as the city of Reykjavik has a plethora of options, when it comes to food. From traditional Nordic dishes to contemporary international meals, the city has an eclectic selection of culinary offerings that will gratify your taste buds and stomach. What's more, the city is abundant in sources for fresh meat and seafood. With its rich and diverse culinary scene, it is no wonder foodies consider this city as their ultimate European destination.

Cheap options

C is for Cookie Restaurant

Known for its nectarous chocolate cakes and delightful hot coffees, the lovely small café boasts a colorful bohemian vibe, friendly staff and above all, affordable tasty treats. Whether you are sipping from a cup of coffee, cappuccino or tea, this café is a great place to relax as well as enjoy a snack during a cold windy day in the city.

- Address: Tysgata 8, Reykjavik, Iceland

- Contact number: +353 578 5914

Nudluskalin Restaurant

Despite its small space, the Nudluskalin Restaurant is considered by many foodies as one the best places to dine in Reykjavik. Not only does it have a cozy and romantic ambiance, but it also serves a variety of hearty noodle meals that are made from fresh produce.

- Skolavordustig 8, Reykjavik 101, Iceland

- +354 562 0202

Ida Zimsen Restaurant

For book lovers, make sure to check out the Ida Zimsen Restaurant in Vesturgata. Located right at the heart of the city, this restaurant is famous for its chilled out atmosphere, sumptuous cakes, high quality coffee, and of course, books.

- Vesturgata 2a, 101 Reykjavik, Iceland

- +354 551 5004

Mid-range

Glo Restaurant

For a healthy and filling vegetarian meal in Reykjavik, head down to Glo Restaurant, an award-winning vegetarian restaurant in Iceland. From veggie wraps to awesome vegan potatoes and pumpkin soup, this restaurant has a load of culinary offerings that will please health-conscious eaters.

- Address: Engjateigur 19, Laugavegur 20b, Reykjavik, Iceland

- Contact number: +354 553 1111

Svarta Kaffi Restaurant

Looking for delicious homemade soups with fresh bread? Then, the Svarta Kaffi Restaurant is your best bet. In addition to its amazing soups and freshly baked bread, it has a terrific setting and is quite affordable compared to other restaurants in the city.

- Address: Laugavegi 54, 101, Reykjavik, Iceland

- Contact number: +354 551 2999

Sjavargrillid Restaurant

Sjavargrillid Restaurant, or also known as Seafood Grill, is hands down one of the finest seafood restaurants in the country. Spearheaded by the world renowned Chef Gustav, this seafood restaurant has a broad menu of adorable seafood staples and Icelandic treats. On top of that, the restaurant has a cozy and warm lodge feel, giving you an unforgettable dining experience.

- Address: Skolavordustigur 14, Reykjavik, Iceland

- Contact number: +354 571 1100

Upscale restaurants

Fridrik V Restaurant

An award-winning upscale restaurant, the Fridrik V Restaurant is arguably Iceland's finest and most beloved Scandinavian restaurant. As a Scandinavian restaurant, Fridrik V offers a bunch of different delectable Scandinavian treats like the duck liver pate. Furthermore, it has a fine selection of bubbly and enticing wines. What else do you need?

- Address: Laugavegur 60, Reykjavik 101, Iceland

- Contact number: +354 461 5775

Kol Restaurant

From service and food quality to interior design, nearly every aspect of the Kol Restaurant is perfect. As a guest in this restaurant, you will be able to savor scrumptious grilled foods as well as tasty international and Delicatessen dishes.

- Skolavordustigur 40, Reykjavik 101, Iceland

- Contact number: +354 517 7474

Dill Restaurant

Upon arrival, the restaurant's staff will give you a cold bottle of delicious complimentary champagne. Afterwards, you will have to pick your meals from a wide selection of Scandinavian, Danish and Swedish dishes. Besides its exceptional culinary offerings, the restaurant boasts a dramatic and comfortable ambiance as well.

- Hverfisgata, Reykjavik 101, Iceland

- Contact number: +354 552 1522

10: BEST PLACES TO CRASH

Hotel Borg Reykjavik. Left Photo credit: <u>Oliver Ruhm</u>.
Right Photo credit: <u>Ryan Rasmussen</u> via Flickr

As Iceland's capital and epicenter of tourism, the city of Reykjavik serves as a home to a cluster of lodging accommodations. From world-class resorts and luxurious boutique hotels to cheap hostels and a campsite, the city also has a diverse mix of accommodations to suit all kinds of travelers. But with a broad pool of accommodations available, how do you pick the best one for you? To help you choose the best place to crash and get a good night's sleep in Reykjavik, take note of the suggestions listed below.

Cheap

Minna-Mosfell Guesthouse

With its tranquil and relaxing feel, the Minna-Mosfell Guesthouse will help you get away from hustle bustle city life. Furthermore, staying here enables you to experience Icelandic hospitality at its finest. As a guest in this B&B, you will be treated with jams as well as freshly made pancakes and bread for breakfast every day.

- Address: Mosfellsbaer, Reykjavik 271, Iceland
- +354 669 0366

Reykjavik Hostel Village

With its convenient location and affordable rates, the Reykjavik Hostel Village has become a favorite respite among budget-conscious travelers and backpackers. Besides its great location, the hostel also has a ton of amazing facilities and amenities, including free parking, Wi-fi, BBQ facilities and a whole lot more.

- Address: Flókagata 1, 105 Reykjavik, Iceland

Reykjavik Backpackers Hostel

The Reykjavik Backpackers Hostel is an amazing budget hostel that truly lives up to its name. Designed for backpackers, this hostel is indeed ideal for those looking for a way cut down their expenses during their trip to Reykjavik. Nestled right at the heart of the city, the hostel also has a good location with the city's best attractions just a few yards away.

- Address: Laugavegur 28, 101 Reykjavik, Iceland

Kex Hostel

No other hostel or hostel in the entire city is as cool and stylish as the Kex Hostel. Famous for its hippy and trendy vibes, the hostel has everything a traveler would need. Not to mention, their staff is courteous, polite and professional.

- Address: Skulagata 28, Reykjavik 101, Iceland

- +354 561 6060

Midrange

Hótel Björk

Set in the midst of the bustling city, Hótel Björk is a lovely hotel just a few minutes away from the city's fabled shopping street, Laugavegur. Known for its cozy and immaculately clean rooms, the hotel has also all the amenities you would need for your stay. In addition, it has an exquisite restaurant that offers a charming blend of international flavors and Icelandic cuisine.

- Address: Brautarholt 22-24, 104 Reykjavik, Iceland

Central Hotel Plaza

Surrounded by wild and intriguing nightlife attractions, the Central Hotel Plaza is the preferred refuge for party goers and nocturnal tourists. Aside from its excellent location, the hotel also has comfortable and spacious rooms with satellite televisions, mini-bars and beautiful wooden floors.

- Address: Adalstraeti 4, 101 Reykjavik, Iceland

Fosshotel Lind

Located conveniently in the midst of Reykjavik, the Fosshotel Lind gives its guests easy access to the city's most celebrated landmarks and attractions, including the striking Hallgrimskirkja Church, Harpa Concert Hall, Sun Voyager sculpture and many more. As for its rooms, the hotel has over 70 well-designed rooms that come with a handful of amenities and facilities.

- Address: Raudararstigur 18, Reykjavik 101, Iceland

Luxurious accommodations

Black Pearl

Often ranked as the top hotel in Reykjavik, Black Pearl is a true of epitome of class and sophistication. Studded with gorgeous apartments, Black Pearl has an opulent and idyllic feel that will give you a slice of heaven on earth. Aside from its classy rooms, the hotel showcases balconies that provide great views of the city.

- Address: Tryggvagata, 18/18c, Reykjavik 101, Iceland

Hotel Borg

Overlooking the iconic Asuturvollur Square, Hotel Borg is an elegant and sleek Art Deco hotel located in the heart of Reykjavik. As an upscale hotel, Hotel Borg offers comfortable premium beds and spacious room embellished in stylish furniture and wooden floors.

- Address: Pósthússtræti 11, 101 Reykjavík

Reykjavik Residences

The Reykjavik Residences is a world-class hotel with stylish accommodations and luxurious amenities like free Wi-Fi, modern kitchen facilities and iPod docking stations. Moreover, it is located a few yards away from the city's trendy and buzzing main shopping street.

- Address: Hverfisgata 21, 101 Reykjavík

11: REYKJAVIK TRAVEL ESSENTIALS

When you travel to a foreign country, especially if you have not been there before, it is good to know some essential things like currency used, what are business hours or how to call someone outside the country. Here are some practical information that you can use when traveling to Reykjavik:

Currency

Currency used in Reykjavik is the Icelandic Krone (ISK). It is pronounced *krona*, which means crown, and it resembles the Danish and the Norwegian Krone. You can use cash in Reykjavik when paying for things, but the locals mostly use credit cards. The Icelandic Krone is the only currency that you can use, since Iceland is not part of the European Union and does not use Euro. However, there are banks and exchange offices in the city and at the airport and ATM mashines where you can withdraw your money easily.

Phone Calls

If someone from Europe is trying to reach you through a land line in Reykjavik, Iceland, they need to enter the country code for Iceland, which is (00)354 and then enter a seven digit number; the first of the 7 digits should be 5 for calling Reykjavik.

If someone is calling you from the USA or Canada, the process is similar however the only difference is that they have to enter different exit code before dialing your number (exit code for USA is 011). The process is the same when it comes to dialing mobile phones, however it is important to note that mobile numbers can have 7 or 9 digits.

To call European countries from Iceland enter 00 followed by the phone number and if you call the USA dial 001 and the rest of the digits. If you are looking for payphones in Reykjavik, it will be hard to find any; as they were removed when the mobile phones took over.

Standard Mealtimes

When it comes to food and mealtimes in Reykjavik, they vary. If you are staying in a hotel, you can expect breakfast buffets to be served 5.00am-10.00am. Lunch is often served from 12.00pm-4.00pm and dinner is usually served around 8.00pm and on the weekends even later.

Business Hours

Business hours in Reykjavik are different usually 09.00am-5.00pm during the winter time, and during the summer month of June, July and August they are 09.00am-4.00pm. When it comes to shopping centers and stores, they are usually open 09.00am-6.00pm on the weekdays and on Saturday 10.00am-1.00/2.00/4.00pm. Shops and stores are generally closed on Sundays however if its food you are after, you can find some supermarkets that work till 11.00pm every day of the week. Banks are open from Monday to Friday 09.15am-4.00pm.

Key Closure Days

In the period of winter holidays, there are a few days when everything is closed or closes much earlier than usual. Most places shut down December 24th or work just till noon. Also, on December 31st everything is closes early and on January 1st you can find few places that are open however, almost everything is closed. Thursday and Friday before Easter and Easter Monday are official holidays in Iceland and everything is closed. Also, Labor Day is celebrated for three days on the first weekend of August as an official holiday and everything is closed on Monday.

12: ICELANDIC LANGUAGE ESSENTIALS

When you are traveling to a foreign country, it is good and useful to know some of the most frequent phrases in their language. They will come in handy for everyday situations, like greetings, looking for directions or when you arrive at the hotel. Here are some of the phrases in Icelandic with pronunciation that you should learn when going to Reykjavik.

Greetings:

Hello. / Halló. (*Hah-low*)

Hello (informal, to a man). / Sæll. (*Sight-l.*)

Hello (informal, to a woman). / Sæl. (*Sigh-l.*)

Goodbye. / Bless. (*Bless*)

Good morning. / Góðan dag. (*Go-den-dog.*)

Good evening. / Gott kvöld. (*Got kvur-lt.*)

Good night. / Góða nótt. (*Goh-dha no-ht.*)

Directions:

How do I get to _____ **?** / Hvernig kemst ég til _____? (*Kver-nik kem-st ye til* _____?)

Where is _____**?** / Hvar er _____? (*Kvar er* _____?)

...the bus stop? / ...strætóstopp? (*...strigh-toh-sto-hp?*)

...the bus station? / ...strætóstöðin? (*...strigh-toh-stur-dhin?*)

...the coach station? / ...biðstöðin? (*...bidh-stur-dhin?*)

...the airport? / ...flugvöllurinn? (*...blu-kvojt-lur-inn?*)

...downtown? ...niður í miðbæ? (*ni-dur ee midh-bye*) "*bye*" like English "Bye"

...the youth hostel? / ...farfuglaheimilið? (*...far-fuk-la-hay-mil-idh?*)

...the guest house? / ...gistihúsið? (*...gi-sti-hoos-idh?*)

Where are there ... / Hvar eru ... (*Kvar eruh...*)

...a lot of hotels? / ...mörg hótel? (*...muhrg hoh-tel?*)

...a lot of restaurants? / ...mörg veitingahús? (*...muhrg vay-tin-ka-hoos?*)

...a lot of bars? / ...margar krár? (*mar-gawr krowr*)

...a lot of sites to see? / ...margir ferðamannastaðir? (*...mahr-gihr fer-dha-man-na-sta-dhir?*)

Can you show me on the map? / Gætiru sýnt mér á kortinu? (*Gai-tiru see-nt m-yer a kort-inu?*)

street / stræti (*strigh-ti*)

turn left / fara til vinstri (*fa-ra til vin-stri*)

turn right / fara til hægri (*fa-ra til high-kri*)

left / vinstri (*vin-stri*)

right / hægri (*high-kri*)

straight ahead / beint áfram (*bay-nt aw-fram*)

north / norður (*nor-dhur*)

south / suður (*su-dhur*)

east / austur (*ur-ee-stur*)

west / vestur (*ve-stur*)

At the Restaurant:

I am hungry./ Èg er svangur.(male) (*Ye-er shvan-gur*) Èg er swöng. (female) (*Ye-er shvung*)

I would like to order. / Èg er tilbúinn að panta. (*Ye-er-tilbooin ad panta*)

May I have the bill, please? / Gæti ég fengið reikninginn? (*Gigh-ti ye fen-kidh-rehnigen*)

Waiter / þjón (thyon)

The food and service were excellent. / Maturinn og þjónustan var frábær. (*Maturin-oh thyonu-stan var frow-ber*)

At the Hotel:

Do you have any rooms available? / Áttu laus herbergi? (*Ow-tu luhys her-ber-ki?*)

I'd like a single/double room. / Gæti ég fengið einsmanns herbergi/tveggjamanna herbergi.(*Gigh-ti ye fen-kidh ay-ns-mans her-ber-ki/tvek-ja-ma-na her-ber-ki.*)

Does the room come with... / Kemur það með... (*Ke-mur thadh medh...*)

...bedsheets? / ...rúmfötum? (*...room-furt-ohm?*)

...a bathroom? / ...klósetti? (*...kloh-se-htee?*)

...a telephone? / ...síma? (*...see-mah?*)

...a TV? / ...sjónvarp? (*...syohn-varpee?*)

...a bath/shower? / ...baði/sturtu? (*...ba-*

dhi/stuhr-tu?)

May I see the room first? / Má ég sjá herbergið fyrst? (*Maw ye syaw her-berg-ith fi-rst?*)

Do you have anything quieter? / Ertu nokkuð með rólegri herbergi? (*Er-tu no-chk-udh medh roh-leg-rih her-ber-ki?*)

...bigger? / ...stærra herbergi? (*...sty-rah her-ber-ki?*)

...cleaner? / ...hreinna herbergi? (*...hraydna her-ber-ki?*)

...cheaper? / ...ódýrara herbergi? (*...oh-deer-a-ra her-ber-ki*)

Social:

Thank you very much. / Takk fyrir (*Tak firir*)

No, thank you. / Nei takk. (*Ney tak*)

Please/ Vinsamlegast (*Vin-sam-le-gast*)

Excuse me. / Fyrirgefðu (*Firir-gef-du*)

How are you? / Hvernig hefur þú það? (*Hver-nig hefur thu-thad*)

What's your name? / Hvað heitir þú? (*Hvad hei-tir thu?*)

My name is.../ Ég heiti... (*Ye-heyti...*)

Where are you from?/ Hvaðan ertu? (*Hva-dan ertu?*)

13: REYKJAVIK'S TOP 20 THINGS TO DO

Reykjavik is a city that offers you various attractions and can satisfy anyone's taste. It is full of natural resources and it has a rich cultural and historical heritage. We bring you the 20 things not miss while in Reykjavik.

Hallgrimskirkja is a stunning church in Skolavorduholti that will take your breath away. It is also the highest building in Reykjavik and people come here mostly for the view that they can catch from the tower. Open hours are from 09.00am-10.00pm(church) and 09.00am-5.00pm(tower).

Runtur is actually a bar crawl that takes places on the weekends. It starts after midnight and it guarantees you a lot of fun. It takes place in Laugavegur and last until early morning hours.

National Museum of Iceland is located in has an impressive collection of artifacts that cover a pretty long period of history. If you want to get to know Iceland's history, this is a place to be. It is located in Sudurgata and open hours are from 10.00am-5.00pm.

http://www.thjodminjasafn.is/

Pearl is a beautiful glass construction with a spinning restaurant inside, a museum and a stunning viewpoint on the 4th floor. It is located on the Öskjuhlíd Hill and the open hours are every day from 10.00am-10.00pm (restaurant is open till 11.00pm)

http://perlan.is/

Vidistadatun Sculpture Park is a park in a lava field, located in the neighborhood of Hafnarfjordur and it has 16 amazing sculptures that were created as a part of the art festivals in 1991 and 1993.

Volcano House is a popular place for tourists; it shows films about volcanoes, has a collection of lava stones and a souvenir shop. It is located in Tryggvagata and open hours are from 10.00am-9.00pm.

Laugardalur is a magnificent park in Engjavegur and a popular place for recreation. It has the largest outdoor thermal pool in the city, a zoo, botanical gardens and a lot of other things to keep you busy.

http://www.visitreykjavik.is/laugardalur-valley

Imagine Peace Tower is a memorial to John Lennon; a beautiful wishing well-shaped construction with colorful lights up in the sky. It is located on Videy Island and it is only lit up on certain days of the year, like John Lennon's and

Yoko Ono's birthday.

http://imaginepeacetower.com/

Grotta Lighthouse is located in a peaceful neighborhood of Seltjarnarnes. It has a great landscape, rich birdlife and the best thing is that it's a perfect place to see the Northern Lights.

Art Museum is located on three different locations in the city; Tryggvagötu, Sigtún and Flókagata. Each of them has different collections from statues, painting and other art works. Open hours vary from one to another, but you can get the information on their official site.

http://www.listasafnreykjavikur.is/

Gullfoss is surely one of the most amazing waterfalls in Iceland, situated on the White River. During the summer, when the sun strikes the falls, it creates a bunch of rainbows making it look like a fairytale place.

http://www.gullfoss.org/

Northern Lights are a "must see" when visiting Reykjavik during the winter months. You don't have to go completely outside of town to see the lights, but if you want to see it in the full darkness, go to the countryside.

Strokkur is a magnificent geyser that blows hot water about 100 feet into the air. You can catch it on camera as it blows water approximately every 5 minutes. It is located in Haukadalsvegur.

http://www.amazingplacesonearth.com/strokkur-iceland/

Whale watching I as popular activity in Iceland and many tourists and whale lovers can't wait to join. You will have a chance to see whales and a few more animal species in their natural habitat.

http://www.specialtours.is/all-tours/whale-watching

Hofsstadir Historic Park is located in Kirkjulundur, about 9 km from the city center. It has a Viking-age longhouse and the whole area dates from that period. You can visit it every day and admission is free.

http://www.nat.is/hofstadir_gardabaer.htm

Bridge Between Continents is an interesting place in Nesvegur. It is "bridge" that connects continents and a place where you get a unique opportunity to cross from Europe to North America by foot.

Solfar Sculpture or the Sun Voyager in Saebraut is an interesting artwork shaped as a Viking ship that can be found on the coastline of Reykjavik.

http://sunvoyageris.com/

Harpa is Reykajavik's concert hall and conference center. It is a stunning building that was even

awarded for its architectural uniqueness. If there is
no event, take an hour or two to wander through
the building, it is worth your time.

http://en.harpa.is/

Thingvellir National Park is an area with a
magnificent landscape and a part of UNESCO
World Heritage. It is a great place for hiking and it
is located about 30 miles east from Reykjavik.

http://www.thingvellir.is/english.aspx

Blue Lagoon is a geothermal spa located in
Grindavik, not too far from Reykjavik. It gives you
the whole spa experience highlighted by the
beautiful landscape. It is open every day from
10.00-20.00.

http://www.bluelagoon.com

CONCLUSION

Whether you are a nocturnal party animal or a nature lover, there is something for you to enjoy in this Nordic haven. From eccentric museums and historic sites to world-class restaurants and bustling nightclubs, a visit to the city of Reykjavik is a magnificent journey that will please all your sense in a myriad of ways. As a tourist hub, it might be as popular as its European neighbors like Paris and Barcelona, Budapest, London and Vienna. Nevertheless, it is a rising star that will soon become a force to be reckoned with, as far as European tourism is concerned. With its peculiar character and diverse mix of attractions, Reykjavik may be soon become one of the world's most sought-after destination.

As you can see, there are a lot of exciting things you can within three days in this European haven. From sightseeing to spine-tingling outdoor trips, the city has an endless array of activities to offer its beloved visitors and guests. If you can't get enough of Reykjavik in three days, extend your stay, and make sure to visit the other attractions of this Nordic utopia. Bless!

MORE FROM THIS AUTHOR

Below you'll find some of our other books that are popular on Amazon and Kindle as well.

Alternatively, you can visit our author page on Amazon to see other work done by us.

3 Day Guide to Berlin: A 72-hour definitive guide on what to see, eat and enjoy in Berlin, Germany

3 Day Guide to Vienna: A 72-hour definitive guide on what to see, eat and enjoy in Vienna Austria

3 Day Guide to Santorini: A 72-hour definitive guide on what to see, eat and enjoy in Santorini Greece

3 Day Guide to Provence: A 72-hour definitive guide on what to see, eat and enjoy in

Provence, France

3 Day Guide to Istanbul: A 72-hour definitive guide on what to see, eat and enjoy in Istanbul, Turkey

3 Day Guide to Budapest: A 72-hour Definitive Guide on What to See, Eat and Enjoy in Budapest, Hungary

20212622R00051

Made in the USA
Middletown, DE
19 May 2015